Washington on Trial

THE PEOPLE OF CUBA VS. THE GOVERNMENT OF THE UNITED STATES OF AMERICA

With an introduction by David Deutschmann and Michael Ratner

OCEAN PRESS
Melbourne • New York

Cover design by David Spratt

Copyright © 1999 Ocean Press

All rights reserved. No part of this publication may be reproduced, stored in a retrieval system or transmitted in any form or by any means, electronic, mechanical, photocopying, recording or otherwise, without the prior permission of the publisher.

ISBN 1-876175-23-0

First printed 1999

Printed in Australia

Published by Ocean Press
Australia: GPO Box 3279, Melbourne, Victoria 3001, Australia
   • Fax: (61-3) 9372 1765 • E-mail: ocean_press@msn.com.au
USA: PO Box 834, Hoboken, NJ 07030 • Fax: 201-617 0203

OCEAN PRESS DISTRIBUTORS
United States: LPC/InBook,
   1436 West Randolph St, Chicago, IL 60607, USA
Canada: Login Brothers
   324 Salteaux Cres, Winnipeg, Manitoba R3J, Canada
Britain and Europe: Global Book Marketing,
   38 King Street, London, WC2E 8JT, UK
Australia and New Zealand: Astam Books,
   57-61 John Street, Leichhardt, NSW 2040, Australia
Cuba and Latin America: Ocean Press,
   Calle 21 #406, Vedado, Havana, Cuba
Southern Africa: Phambili Agencies,
   PO Box 28680, Kensington 2101, Johannesburg, South Africa

Introduction

On May 31, 1999, eight organizations representing the Cuban people issued a lawsuit against the Government of the United States. The claim seeks a total of $181.1 billion in damages for the loss of life and human injury as a result of U.S. acts of aggression against Cuba over the past 40 years. The lawsuit was filed at the Civil and Administrative Court of Law at the Provincial People's Court in Havana City.

Cuba has based this claim on war crimes such as the Bay of Pigs invasion, the use of biological warfare, bombings and air attacks, military provocations from the U.S. Naval Base at Guantánamo, and support for terrorist actions.

The Cuban legal action — with social and mass organizations comprising almost the entire Cuban population as the plaintiffs — has named the U.S. Government as the defendant in the claim. The lawsuit seeks compensation for the lives of 3,478 Cubans and injuries to a further 2,099 Cubans as a result of U.S. military aggression against the island.

The Cuban lawsuit is made on behalf of eight popular organizations that comprise a major part of the Cuban population: Central Trade Union of Cuba (CTC), National Association of Small Farmers (ANAP), Federation of Cuban Women (FMC), Federation of University Students (FEU), Federation of Middle Level Education Students (FEEM), José Martí Children's Organization, Committees for the Defense of the Revolution (CDR), and the Association of Combatants of the Cuban Revolution (ACRC).

The Cuban lawsuit asserts the following:

- That the covert operations organized in Washington against Cuba began in the summer of 1959.
- That the U.S. Government planned and supported bands of armed terrorists on the island — described by the Cubans as bandits — beginning in 1960 and lasting five years until 1965.

- That the U.S. Government initiated and organized the Bay of Pigs invasion of April 17, 1961.
- That the U.S. Government has made permanent use of terrorism as an instrument of its foreign policy against Cuba.
- That the U.S. Naval Base at Guantánamo — still maintained by the United States against the wishes of Cuba — has been used by the U.S. Government to both shelter criminal fugitives as well as to initiate provocations and acts of terror against Cuba.
- That the U.S. Government has used biological warfare against the Cuban people, citing the example of the deliberate introduction to Cuba in 1981 of the dengue-2 virus.
- That Cuba has faced — and still does — the constant danger of direct military aggression from the United States.
- That this threat of constant military aggression from its nearest neighbor imposes a great economic and psychological burden on Cuba and its people, forcing it to maintain a permanent military alert.

It is not without significance that this lawsuit was initiated shortly after the 40th anniversary of the Cuban Revolution. Few countries have been subjected to such an unrelenting attempt to subvert its internal rule in the way that Cuba has endured since January 1959. It can only be described as an undeclared war, that has now lasted some four decades.

This lawsuit highlights what could be described as the military aspect of this undeclared war by the United States against Cuba. It seeks formal compensation for the damage to human life — both the loss of life and physical injury. Not presently claimed by Cuba are the less tangible but no less devastating psychological effects of a whole people having to live with the fear of invasion and armed assault for most of these past 40 years. Nor is Cuba presently claiming the crippling economic effects of the ever-tightening economic blockade imposed by the United States against Cuba. Finally, absent from this present lawsuit is a compensation claim by Cuba for the repeated and numerous attempts by the U.S. Government — well documented by the U.S. Senate itself — to assassinate Fidel Castro and other leaders of the Cuban Government.

The evolution of U.S. foreign policy in the four decades since the triumph of the Cuban revolution has been described as a "textbook instance of the gap between the abstractions of contemporary International Law and the concrete realities of geopolitics".[1] For more than a century, the United States has asserted its historical claim to control the political destinies of the hemisphere. In the language of geopolitics, Cuba — since the beginning of its existence as a neo-colony in the aftermath of the Cuban-Spanish-American War in 1898 — has found itself within a U.S. sphere of influence and as such has experienced severe economic exploitation reinforced by periodic military interventions, including several carried out before the 1959 revolution. During the last several decades, any country in the Caribbean and Central American region that has repudiated U.S. supremacy has quickly become a target of military intervention, including Guatemala (1954), the Dominican Republic (1965), Nicaragua (1980s), Grenada (1983) and Panama (1989), to mention the most obvious examples.

Cuba, too, was subjected to a direct military intervention initiated and led by the United States — the Bay of Pigs invasion of 1961. The training and financing of Cuban exiles for a military expedition of the sort that eventuated at the Bay of Pigs was illegal under International Law, as were the CIA operations that included plots to assassinate Cuban government leaders — even recruiting Mafia operatives as contract killers — and the repeated attempts to undermine the Cuban constitutional order by various subversive programs.

The record of the United States on the use of force remains self serving. Although it formally champions a prohibition of use of force, the United States has made a series of exceptions to justify its own frequent military interventions. It insists on defining for itself what constitutes aggression and what constitutes self-defense, and has relied on an "elastic conception"[2] of defensive force that includes repeated recourse to military intervention in its relations with the Third World. The U.S. Government has refused to accept the authority of the United Nations or even the International Court of Justice when its own use of force is questioned, as was the case in

---

[1] Richard Falk, "Introduction" in Michael Krinsky and David Golove (eds), *United States Economic Measures Against Cuba: Proceedings in the United Nations and International Law Issues*, 7.
[2] Ibid.

the 1986 decision of the International Court of Justice that found illegal the principal U.S. efforts to destabilize the FSLN government of Nicaragua. In addition, the United States has maintained and relied upon the covert operations of the CIA to distort the constitutional processes of other countries and evade the prohibition on aggression.[3]

The United States hides behind the "national security versus international law" debate, with the intention of providing an escape clause for Washington. Normally not presented in such a candid manner, this was the view of former U.S. Secretary of State Dean Acheson, who made this observation in the aftermath of the 1962 Cuban Missile Crisis and the naval blockade of Cuba imposed by the United States:

> I must conclude that the propriety of the Cuban [naval] quarantine is not a legal issue. The power, prestige and position of the United States had been challenged by another state; and law simply does not deal with such questions of power — power that comes close to the sources of sovereignty. I cannot believe that there are principles of law that say we must accept destruction of our way of life... No law can destroy the state creating the law. The survival of states is not a matter of law.[4]

This view asserts that the "survival" of the United States has been threatened by Cuba and that this places U.S. policy toward Cuba outside the restraints of International Law. How can this be defended? How can Washington claim that the island of Cuba and its 10 million inhabitants pose a military threat to the survival of the United States? In the name of defending its "way of life," the United States is willing to threaten the survival of other sovereign states — witness its policy toward Cuba during these past four decades — without being subject to the legal boundaries that are said to govern the conduct of the rest of the world community.

Under International Law all states are free to select the government of their choice. It is beyond the jurisdiction of international organizations, or of any state for that matter, to determine the internal social, political and economic structures of a sovereign

---

[3] Ibid.
[4] Dean Acheson, *New York Times* (New York), 10 December 1964.

state. This principle is reinforced in the Charter of the United Nations and has been reaffirmed in numerous international agreements and resolutions of international organizations. The International Court of Justice, for example, has articulated the principle of non-intervention and the sovereign right of states. The Court has held that the principle of non-intervention had become a fundamental norm of International Law and was the basis for the orderly working of present day international society.

Up to the present, most legal action in the U.S.-Cuba conflict has been initiated by the United States against Cuba. This lawsuit on behalf of Cuban social and mass organizations does something both extraordinary and necessary: It puts Washington on trial. The Cuban claim for compensation against the U.S. Government allows Cuba the opportunity to present before the international community its evidence — frequently based on declassified U.S. Government documents — that Washington has a case to answer.

This booklet was produced in great haste, with the purpose of distributing the Statement of Claim as widely as possible. Mirta Muñiz, director of the Havana office of Ocean Press, was particularly helpful in coordinating the project. The subheads used throughout the Claim have been added by the publisher. The annexes to the Statement of Claim will be included in an expanded book on the Cuban lawsuit that is in preparation and to be published by Ocean Press.

David Deutschmann
Michael Ratner
June 1999

THE PEOPLE OF CUBA VS. THE GOVERNMENT OF THE UNITED STATES OF AMERICA FOR HUMAN DAMAGES

TO BE SUBMITTED TO THE CIVIL AND ADMINISTRATIVE COURT OF LAW AT THE PROVINCIAL PEOPLE'S COURT IN HAVANA CITY

Attorney Juan Mendoza Díaz, attorney Leonardo B. Pérez Gallardo, attorney Magaly Iserne Carrillo and attorney Ivonne Pérez Gutiérrez, on behalf of and representing the following social and mass organizations from the Republic of Cuba comprising almost the entire population in the country:

1. **Central Trade Union of Cuba (CTC)**, represented by worker **Pedro Ross Leal**, a Social Sciences graduate and Secretary General of the organization.
2. **National Association of Small Farmers (ANAP)**, represented by farmer **Orlando Lugo Fonte**, a Social Sciences graduate and chairman of the organization.
3. **Federation of Cuban Women (FMC)**, represented by chemical engineer **Vilma Espín Guillois**, president of the organization.
4. **Federation of University Students (FEU)**, represented by **Carlos Manuel Valenciaga Díaz**, recently graduated from "Enrique José Varona" Higher Pedagogical Institute, leader of the organization.
5. **Federation of Middle-level Education Students (FEEM)**, represented by **Yurima Blanco García**, a senior student at "Amadeo Roldán" Provincial Music School, leader of the organization.
6. **"José Martí" Children's Organization**, represented by **Niurka Dumenigo García**, a Social Communication major, leader of the organization's National Board.

7. **Committees for the Defense of the Revolution (CDR)**, represented by **Juan Contino Aslan**, an accountancy graduate and national coordinator of the organization.
8. **Association of Combatants of the Cuban Revolution (ACRC)**, represented by Commander of the Revolution **Juan Almeida Bosque**, president of the organization.

Hereby, by deed we appear and according to rule we say:

That, we have come to institute a Claim against the **Government of the United States of America** in Ordinary Proceeding on Compensation for Damages.

That, this Claim is based on the following:

FACTS

COVERT WAR BEGAN IN 1959

FIRST: That, the triumph of the Cuban Revolution on January 1, 1959, meant for the people of Cuba — for the first time in its long history of struggle — the conquest of true independence and sovereignty. A death toll of about 20,000 people perished in direct and heroic combat against the forces of [Batista's] military dictatorship, which were trained, equipped and advised by the Government of the United States.

The revolutionary victory in Cuba was one of the most humiliating political defeats the United States sustained after it became a great imperialist power. This meant that the historical dispute between the two nations would enter a new and more acute stage of confrontation. This new stage of confrontation was characterized by the implementation of a brutal policy of hostility and aggression emanating from the United States and aimed at the destruction of the Cuban Revolution. The objective of this policy was the recapture of the country and the return to the neo-colonial system of domination that it had imposed on Cuba for over a century and which it definitively lost over 40 years ago.

The war unleashed by the United States against the Cuban Revolution, conceived as a state policy, has been historically proven and can be fully confirmed by widespread information recently released in the United States. This documentation shows a number of political, military, economic, biological, diplomatic, psychological, propagandist and spying actions; the execution of acts of terrorism and sabotage; the organization and logistical support of armed bandits and clandestine groups of mercenaries; the encouragement of defection and migration; and the attempts at the physical elimination of the leaders of the Cuban revolutionary process.

All this has been exposed in very significant public statements made by senior officials of the U.S. Government as well as in the extensive and irrefutable evidence accumulated by the Cuban authorities. Also, numerous declassified secret documents are particularly eloquent, and although not all have been released, those that already have been released suffice to prove the grounds for this claim.

One of the annexed documents which confirms the events described is the already declassified "Program of Covert Actions Against the Castro Regime," approved on March 17, 1960, by U.S. President Dwight D. Eisenhower. The second annexed document, entitled "The Cuba Project" and introduced on January 18, 1962, by Brigade General Edward Lansdale to the highest echelons of the U.S. Government and the National Security Council Special Group-Augmented, contains the list of 32 covert actions to be carried out by the agencies and departments taking part in the so-called Operation Mongoose.

Every hostile act of aggression carried out by the U.S. Government against Cuba from the very triumph of the Revolution up to the present have caused enormous material and human losses and incalculable suffering to the people of this country as well as hardships resulting from the shortage of medication, food and other indispensable means of life which we deserve and have the right to obtain with our honest labor.

Likewise, the political and ideological subversion which resulted in continual, extensive and unjustified distress endured by all the people has posed constant dangers and caused pervasive and almost immeasurable damages. This has jeopardized an accurate assessment which we are not including at this time for the purpose of this Claim in order to strictly limit ourselves to the content of the restitution for moral damages as prescribed by the Cuban Civil Code presently in force, although we do not renounce our right to do so in due course.

Pursuant to international practice, a State is responsible for the damages caused by its behavior and actions — in legislative as well as in administrative and judicial terms — by its agents and officials, and even for the actions of each country's natural persons, if the corresponding authorities in the said State avoid taking preventive or suppressive measures. Thus, it is its duty to compensate for such damages in compliance with what is universally regarded as civil liability.

Accordingly, the United States of America, as a State represented by its Government, is accountable for the damages caused to Cuban natural persons and legal entities due to the unlawful actions undertaken by its agencies, departments, representatives, officials or the government itself.

AIR ATTACKS

SECOND: That, the recent declassification in the United States of a report produced by Central Intelligence Agency (CIA) Inspector General Lyman Kirkpatrick on October 1961, with a review of the reasons for the failure of the Bay of Pigs invasion — as it is called in America — has revealed that the covert operations organized in Washington against Cuba began in the summer of 1959, a few weeks after the adoption of the Land Reform Law on May 17 of that year.

In the month of October [1959], President Eisenhower approved a program proposed by the Department of State and the CIA to undertake covert actions against Cuba, including air and naval pirate attacks and the promotion of, and direct support to, counter-revolutionary groups inside Cuba. According to the document, the operations were to have succeeded in making the overthrow of the revolutionary regime look like the result of its own mistakes.

Those days saw the beginning of a campaign of flights over Cuban territory by small aircraft coming from the United States with such missions as the infiltration of agents, weapons and other equipment and the realization of acts of sabotage, bombings and other acts of terrorism.

On October 11, 1959, a plane dropped two incendiary bombs on the *Niágara* sugar mill in Pinar del Río province. On October 19, another two bombs were hurled from the air over the *Punta Alegre* sugar mill in Camagüey province. On October 21, a twin-engine aircraft machine-gunned the city of Havana, killing several people and injuring dozens while another light aircraft dropped subversive propaganda. On October 22, a passenger train was machine-gunned in Las Villas province. On October 26, two light aircraft attacked both the *Niágara* and *Violeta* sugar mills.

From the very month of January 1960, while that year's sugar harvest was in full swing, the number of flights over sugarcane plantations multiplied. On January 12 alone, 500,000 *arrobas* [one arroba equals 25 pounds] of sugar cane were set on fire from the air in Havana province. On January 30, over 50,000 *arrobas* were lost at the *Chaparra* sugar mill in the former province of Oriente and, on February 1, more than 100,000 *arrobas* were set alight in Matanzas province.

Still other air attacks would follow: on January 21, a plane dropped four 100-pound bombs over the urban areas of Cojimar and Regla, in the nation's capital. On February 7, 1960, a light plane set afire 1.5 million *arrobas* of sugarcane in the *Violeta, Florida, Céspedes* and *Estrella* sugar mills in Camagüey province.

On February 18, a plane that was bombing the *España* sugar mill in Matanzas province was destroyed in mid air by one of its own bombs. The pilot was identified as Robert Ellis Frost, an American citizen. The flight card registered the plane's departure from Tamiami airport in Florida. Other documents found on the corpse revealed that on three previous occasions the pilot had taken part in similar flights over Cuba.

On February 23, several light aircraft sprayed incendiary capsules over the *Washington* and *Ulacia* sugar mills in the former province of Las Villas, as well as over Manguito in Matanzas province. On March 8, another light aircraft dropped inflammable substances over the area of San Cristóbal and set alight more than 250,000 *arrobas* of sugarcane.

At that stage, along with the bombing, strafing and burning missions, there were successive flights over Havana and almost every other province in the country with the aim of spreading subversive propaganda. Dozens of such flights were recorded just in the first three months of 1961. In the aforementioned report by Lyman Kirkpatrick on the Bay of Pigs invasion, it was stated that "at the time of the invasion, 12 million pounds of leaflets had been dropped over Cuba," leaflets containing counterrevolutionary propaganda. In his report, the high-ranking CIA officer described

the steps that had been taken from August 1959 by a paramilitary group from that institution.
This is but an example. The covert war against Cuba had begun, with high intensity, in the year 1959 itself. An infinite number of hostile and aggressive actions, impossible to list in detail, would follow in the coming years.
The Inspector General of the Central Intelligence Agency recognized that "from January 1960, when it had 40 people, the branch expanded to 588 by April 16, 1961, becoming one of the largest branches in the Clandestine Services." He was referring to the CIA station in Miami which concentrated on activities against Cuba.

ARMED TERRORIST GROUPS
THIRD: That, barely 15 months after the revolutionary victory [on January 1, 1959], armed banditry was planned and finally unleashed by the U.S. Government, practically throughout the length of Cuba. It began in 1960 under the Republican administration of President Eisenhower and lasted five years until 1965.
Its main thrust would be in the Escambray region in the former province of Las Villas, which now comprises the provinces of Villa Clara, Cienfuegos and Sancti Spiritus. A so-called front operated in that zone with columns, bands and a command post. Weeks before the Bay of Pigs mercenary invasion, 40,000 workers and students from the nation's capital, supported by local forces from the central region and peasants and farm workers from the Escambray and organized in militia battalions, surrounded and rendered helpless that bulwark which was to have cooperated with the invasion forces. Hundreds of bandits were captured and their number reduced to a minimum in those critical days.
Those terrorists, organized by the CIA, had the support of the United States government which made the greatest efforts and resorted to every possible means to supply them with weaponry, ammunition, explosives, communication equipment and general logistics. To this end, the U.S. Government used different routes by air, by sea and even via diplomatic channels through the United States embassy in Havana, until relations were severed at the beginning of 1961.
In this respect, the previously mentioned report by the CIA Inspector General explicitly recognized the logistical support

provided by that institution to the mercenary bands. One example is the so-called Operation Silence, which consisted of the U.S. Central Intelligence Agency carrying out 12 air operations between September 1960 and March 1961 in order to supply the bandits with arms, ammunition, explosives and other equipment. About this operation the author of the report stated: "In all, about 151,000 pounds of arms, ammunition and equipment were transported by air."

On September 29, 1960, a four-engine plane dropped a cache of weapons over the Escambray mountains, near the Hanabanilla waterfall. On November 7, a plane dropped another cache of arms over the area of Boca Chica, near El Condado village on the Escambray mountain range. On December 31, another package was dropped over the area known as Pinalillo, between Sagua and La Mulata, in Cabañas in Pinar del Río province. On January 6, 1961, an aircraft dropped 20 parachutes with arms, ammunition, explosives and communication equipment between El Condado and Magua, in Trinidad, Las Villas province. On January 7, the following day, an aircraft dropped American weapons between Cabañas and Bahía Honda, Pinar del Río.

On February 6, a plane dropped 30 parachutes with arms, ammunition, explosives, communication equipment and food over the area of Santa Lucía in Cabaiguán, Las Villas province. On February 13, another 20 parachutes were dropped from a plane over the area of El Naranjo, in Cumanayagua, Las Villas. On February 17, a plane dropped 13 parachutes between San Blas and Circuito Sur, near La Sierrita, Las Villas. On March 3, a plane dropped two cache of arms, ammunition and explosives in the areas of El Mamey and Charco Azul, both in Las Villas province. On March 29, there was another drop of arms and supplies over the Jupiter farm in Artemisa municipality, Pinar del Río province. In other words, a total of more than 70 tons of weapons were sent by air in that period.

Significant pockets of subversion were created in the provinces of Pinar del Río, Havana, Matanzas, Camagüey and Oriente. It is worth emphasizing that the first group was organized in the province of Pinar del Río, led by Luis Lara Crespo, a former corporal with Batista's tyranny army who was a fugitive from the revolutionary justice for his crimes. It was in that same province, that Rebel Army private Manuel Cordero Rodríguez was killed in action against a group of bandits commanded by American citizens Austin Young and Peter John Lambton. These two men were captured along with the rest of the bandits, and their weapons — part of those supplied by the United States — were seized.

These mercenary groups were to be succeeded by others. It is equally useful to highlight those headed by Pedro Román Trujillo in the Escambray region and Olegario Charlot Pileta in the former province of Oriente, both were also among the first groups created in those provinces.

Faced with these expressions of mounting aggression orchestrated by the U.S. Government, the Cuban people — through their defense and security institutions and revolutionary organizations — were actively and resolutely mobilized. They dealt sensitive blows to the enemy and captured, dispersed or dismantled most of the bandits, thus writing pages of heroism and sacrifice with their own blood and the loss of many precious lives.

This situation was not correctly assessed by the CIA, which assumed that the mercenary invasion would have the support of these forces. However, after the historic defeat it persisted in its plans of a dirty war. Under the administrations of Presidents John F. Kennedy and Lyndon B. Johnson, the CIA multiplied its efforts to that end, so there was a resurgence of bands which forced our people to pay an additional toll in blood and lives.

The unquestionable historical truth about these events and the cynicism and lies that have invariably accompanied all American actions against Cuba can be found in the original documents of the time, produced by those who planned the policy of aggression and subversion against Cuba from within that country. By this token, it may be illustrative for this Court that, on March 17, 1960, the U.S. President approved the so-called Program of Covert Action Against the Castro Regime proposed by the CIA. This meeting was attended by Vice-President Richard Nixon, Secretary of State Christian Herter, Secretary of the Treasury Robert B. Anderson, Assistant-Secretary of Defense John N. Irwin, Under-Secretary of State Livingston T. Merchant, Assistant-Secretary of State Roy Rubottom, Admiral Arleigh Burke of the Joint Chiefs of Staff, CIA Director Allen Dulles, the high-ranking CIA officers Richard Bissell and J.C. King and the White House officials Gordon Gray and General Andrew J. Goodpaster.

Among other things, that program enabled the creation of a secret intelligence and action organization within Cuba, for which the CIA allocated the necessary funds. In a recently declassified memorandum on that meeting, General Goodpaster noted: "The President said that he knows of no better plan for dealing with this situation. The great problem is leakage and breach of security. Everyone must be prepared to swear that he [Eisenhower] has not heard of it. [...] He said our hand should not show in anything that is done."

One of the most impressive achievements of social justice in our country has been in the field of education. This has been highly appreciated by our people and enjoys admiration and respect in the world. The literacy campaign was undertaken in 1961. Almost 100,000 students joined it and went to the most remote places on our island to teach reading and writing to the people there. At the same time, the CIA directed its bandits to sow terror in order to sabotage the campaign. Those bandits carried out criminal actions against adolescents and youths working as teachers and against illiterate adults learning to read and write.

On January 5, 1961, voluntary teacher Conrado Benítez García and peasant Eliodoro Rodríguez Linares were murdered in Las Tinajitas, San Ambrosio, Trinidad municipality in Sancti Spiritus. The participants in this action were bandits Macario Quintana Carrero, Julio Emilio Carretero Escajadillo and Ruperto Ulacia Montelier, members of Osvaldo Ramírez García's band. On October 3, that same year, teacher Delfín Sen Cedré was murdered at Novoa farm, Quemado de Güines, in Las Villas by Margarito Lanza Flórez's band.

On November 26, 1961, the young literacy tutor Manuel Ascunce Domenech and peasant Pedro Lantigua Ortega were likewise murdered by bandits Julio Emilio Carretero, Pedro González Sánchez and Braulio Amador Quesada, at Palmarito farm, Rio Ay, Trinidad municipality, in Sancti Spiritus.

Children and adolescents also became the victims of those bandits intent on sowing terror among peasants and farm workers in Cuba. Such is the case, among others, of Yolanda and Fermín Rodríguez Díaz, aged 11 and 13 years. They were murdered on January 24, 1963, at La Candelaria farm, Bolondrón, Pedro Betancourt municipality, in Matanzas province, by Juan José Catalá Coste's band, operating in the south of that province. It is also worthwhile mentioning for its cruelty, the event of March 13, 1962, in San Nicolás de Bari, Havana province, where a youngster named Andrés Rojas Acosta was hanged with the very rope he was using to tie up a pig. This crime was committed by bandits led by mercenary Waldemar Hernández. Another event occurred on October 10, 1960, on the road from Madruga to Ceiba Mocha when Gerardo Fundora's band shot at a passing jeep killing 22-months-old Reynaldo Núñez-Bueno Machado. The baby's mother was also a victim of this action.

The mercenary bands, in a desperate attempt to succeed in their task, retaliated against the civilian population in the areas where they operated. An example of this is the murder of 10-year-old Albinio Sánchez Rodríguez on March 4, 1963. He was killed by Delio Almeida's band as a reaction to a previous attack by the National Revolutionary Militias.

Banditry was definitively removed from Cuba in 1965, when the last band was located and defeated. That band was led by Juan Alberto Martínez Andrade, then leader of the so-called Camagüey Front.

Between 1959 and 1965, a total of 299 bands with 3,995 mercenaries operated throughout the national territory in the service of the U.S. Government.

The number of casualties in that struggle — regular troops and militia combined taking part in the operations against the bandits, as well as people murdered by the bandits whose death it has been possible to document — were as high as 549. Also, a considerable number of people were injured — a number it has not been possible to accurately determine some 34 years later, when this Claim was prepared. However, there are still 200 survivors incapacitated as a result of those criminal plans. Not all the victims were among the revolutionary combatants fighting the bandits. Many civilians who had nothing to do with the military activities also died, victims of the crimes committed by the groups of bandits infiltrated from abroad.

The dirty war, that costly and bloody form of aggression created by the U.S. Government, was definitively and completely defeated by the Cuban people, totally uprooted, and the CIA could never again organize a single band.

We have attached to this Claim the corresponding certificates of the 549 people who have so far been registered as dead due to that criminal action against our people, as well as a detailed list of all those currently incapacitated due to injuries sustained in the period described; these are the documents numbered as 9 and 10, respectively.

BAY OF PIGS

FOURTH: That, among the most significant events in the history of the Cuban Revolution — for its military, patriotic and political impact — is the Bay of Pigs mercenary invasion organized by the U.S. Central Intelligence Agency on instructions given by President Eisenhower on March 17, 1960.

President Eisenhower himself wrote in his memoirs: "On March 17, 1960 [...] I ordered the Central Intelligence Agency to begin to organize the training of the Cuban exiles, mainly in Guatemala."

As part of the preparation for the invasion, the airports at Ciudad Libertad, San Antonio de los Baños and Santiago de Cuba were bombed at dawn on April 15, 1961. The aggression was repelled and, although some planes from the Cuban defense forces were destroyed, they could not render useless our small, recently established Revolutionary Air Force. This was thanks to the courageous performance of the anti-aircraft artillery made up almost entirely of young people who would play an extraordinary role only two days later. Twelve of those youths lost their lives, including Eduardo García Delgado, who entered the history of that epic struggle when he wrote Fidel's name, with his own blood on a board, as he lay dying.

Two days later, on April 17, 1961, at 2:30 in the morning, a group began to land on the southern coast of the former province of Las Villas, at Ciénaga de Zapata. The group had come from Puerto Cabezas in the Republic of Nicaragua. It was organized, trained, equipped and financed by the U.S. Government. Its own members called it Assault Brigade 2506 and it was made up of about 1,500 men.

According to documents seized from those who were taken prisoners, the mercenary invasion plan contemplated landing at three places in Ciénaga de Zapata: Playa Larga, which they called Playa Roja in their plans, where those on board the ship named *Aguja* were to disembark; Playa Girón, called Playa Azul, where the vessels known as *Ballena* and *Tiburón* were to disembark their passengers; and Caleta Verde, called Playa Verde, where those on board ships *Marsopa, Barracuda* and *Atun* were to disembark.

At the same time, two battalions of parachutists would occupy positions in the vicinity of the *Australia* sugar mill, also at San Blas and Soplillar, their mission being to cut off access to the landing and operation zone, then to isolate it, to fortify it and to establish a provisional government there. This would have created the conditions for immediately airlifting to Cuba a government impatiently waiting in Miami with its luggage ready that would request a military intervention by the United States of America at the head of the OAS "troops."

During the invasion, the members of this "government" were forcibly kept incommunicado in the territory of the United States while the CIA issued one statement after another in their name.

The mercenary brigade landed at Playa Girón and Playa Larga despite the resistance put up by small units of the National Revolutionary Militias. They landed their tanks and armored vehicles and dropped the parachutists' battalion north of Playa Girón in order to block the paved road leading to the *Australia* sugar mill. B-26 planes disguised with Cuban insignia and escorted by American fighter planes began bombing the area, strafing the civilian population, killing people — including women and children whose full names can be found at the end of this document — and causing considerable damage.

American Navy units — including an aircraft-carrier (the *Essex*, with 40 fighter planes and a marine battalion on board), a helicopter-carrier, five destroyers and one LSD [Landing Ship Dock] among other naval units — escorted the ships that transported the mercenary forces and remained a few miles off the operation zone throughout the whole battle.

The mercenary brigade had plenty of equipment and weaponry. It had five transport gunboats, two modified LCI artillery war units, three LCV landing craft for transporting heavy equipment and four LCVP troop-carrier landing craft. For air operations, the mercenaries were backed by 16 B-26 fighter planes, six C-46, eight C-54 transport planes and two Catalina seaplanes. They had five M-41 Sherman tanks, with 76-millimeter guns; 10 armored cars equipped with .50-caliber machine-guns; 75 bazookas; 60 mortars of different caliber; 21 recoilless cannons, 75-millimeter and 57-millimeter; 44 machine-guns .50-caliber and 39 light and heavy machine-guns .30-caliber; eight flame-throwers; 22,000 handgrenades; 108 Browning automatic rifles; 470 M-3 submachine-guns; 635 Garand rifles and M-1 carbines; 465 pistols and other light weapons.

The members of the mercenary brigade received military training from American instructors at bases in the United States, Guatemala and Puerto Rico. They received monthly allowances to support their families provided by the U.S. Government, which spent a total of $45 million to finance the operation.

In less than 72 hours, the Cuban revolutionary forces overwhelmingly crushed the powerful invading mercenary brigade. In this respect, the White House issued an official statement on April 24, 1961, where it indicated that, "President Kennedy has stated from the beginning that as President he bears sole responsibility for the invasion." The statement added that "the President is strongly opposed to anyone, within or without the administration, attempting to shift the responsibility."

The U.S. Government's association with the events described in this document was also corroborated in the well-known report by the CIA Inspector General, elaborated six months after the failed invasion. This document had remained classified "top secret" for 37 years until 1998 when it was declassified following intense efforts by the National Security Archive, a non-profit organization based in Washington, D.C.

Although the Bay of Pigs invasion was a major political and military defeat for the government of the United States, this military conflict left a high number of victims and countless grieving or badly afflicted Cuban families. A total of 176 people died and over 300 were wounded by enemy weapons. This included people living in the area who were machine-gunned by the mercenary air force; 50 of them were permanently incapacitated. We verify this with certificates that have been attached to this Claim as documents marked numbers 12 and 13, respectively.

Pilots, advisers, frogmen and other Americans were directly involved in action. In the violent engagements of April 19 [1961], the active participation of American pilots was confirmed when the anti-aircraft forces brought down a B-26 plane piloted by American citizens Thomas Willard Ray and Frank Leo Baker, National Guard pilots in the state of Alabama. On that same day, another B-26 was brought down over the sea. It was piloted by Ryley W. Shamburger and Wade Carroll Gray, the former an officer with the U.S. National Guard.

TERRORIST ACTS

FIFTH: That, terrorism has permanently been used by the United States as an instrument of its foreign policy against Cuba.

One of the U.S. Government's first acts of terrorism against our country was a monstrous crime: the sabotage of the French vessel *La Coubre* on March 4, 1960, at a pier in the port of Havana. In Europe, the boat had loaded a significant shipment of weaponry and ammunition purchased from Belgium by Cuba's revolutionary government, which was already concerned at the growing acts of aggression by the United States.

The cargo was sabotaged by CIA agents at the port of shipment; the devices they planted exploded that day while the ship was unloaded. The bombs were placed with great sophistication, so that there would be a second explosion while the victims of the first one were receiving assistance. Both the ship and the neighboring pier were crowded with port workers, rescue personnel and soldiers who, regardless of the danger, had gone to there to help the victims of the disaster and prevent accidents.

This act of terrorism left 101 dead, including six French sailors, and hundreds of wounded. Now, so many years after the event, it is impossible to give the exact number of the wounded because they were cared for in various hospitals and health care centers in the nation's capital.

The modes of terrorism used against Cuba have mainly been the following: sabotage or destruction of civilian targets inside the country; pirate attacks against coastal facilities, merchant vessels and fishing boats; attacks against Cuban staff and facilities abroad, including diplomatic missions, airline offices and aircraft; and the constant incitement of subversive elements, through radio and television stations, to carry out acts of this nature against production and service centers, even with indications of how to do so.

If our country has been a constant target of terrorist actions during these 40 years of Revolution, it was in 1961 that they became more systematic as a result of the covert action program against Cuba approved on March 17, 1960, by U.S. President Dwight D.

Eisenhower. In the aforementioned now declassified secret document on the program of covert action against Cuba, followed up later by President Kennedy, Eisenhower specified that "the method of accomplishing this end will be to induce, support and, so far as possible, direct action by selected groups of Cubans, both inside and outside of Cuba. These actions will be of a sort that they might be expected to and could undertake on their own initiative."

It was precisely one of these "selected groups" that, on the afternoon of April 13, 1961, set fire to and completely destroyed El Encanto, the biggest department store in the country. This action was carried out by Carlos L. González Vidal, a member of a terrorist group known by the abbreviation MRP [People's Revolutionary Movement]. It was also discovered that the main organizer was Mario Pombo Matamoros, who was in contact with leaders of the M-30-11 group. The consequences of this fire were not only economic but more painful still due to the death of worker Fe del Valle Ramos, plus burns and injuries sustained by 18 other people among the hundreds of employees in the store.

A month before, on March 13, 1961, as part of these same terrorist plans there had been an attack on the Hermanos Díaz oil refinery in Santiago de Cuba, where 27-year-old sailor René Rodríguez Hernández, on sentry duty, was killed and 19-year-old Roberto Ramón Castro was seriously injured. This action was carried out by a CIA commando unit in a gunboat equipped with heavy machine-guns which had been launched from the American ship *Barbara J.*, as described by CIA Inspector General Lyman Kirkpatrick in his report.

On May 28, 1961, some terrorists set alight the Riego cinema in Pinar del Río city, during a children's show. Twenty-six children and 14 adults were injured.

On September 5, 1963, two twin-engine aircraft dropped explosives over the city of Santa Clara, causing the death of teacher Fabric Aguilar Noriega and injuring three of his four children.

On December 23, 1963, a CIA commando unit transported by sea from the United States, using underwater demolition devices, sank the Revolutionary Navy's LT-385 torpedo boat in Siguanea dock on the Isle of Pines, killing second lieutenant Leonardo Luberta Noy and midshipmen Jesús Mendoza Larosa, Fe de la Caridad Hernández Jubón and Andrés Gavilla Soto.

Dozens of similar cases could be listed that occurred in those years.

Plane hijackings, unprecedented in the world, were devised and used by the CIA in its program of terrorist actions against Cuba from 1959. Many such actions took place, especially during the early years of the Revolution. Some took on dramatic characteristics. As an example, we will relate what happened on March 27, 1966, when an unscrupulous individual, Angel Maria Betancourt Cueto, using a firearm, tried to divert to the United States — where they were always welcomed as heroes — an Ilyushin-18 Cubana Airlines plane en route from Santiago de Cuba to Havana, with 97 people on board, including 14 children. Seeing his plan thwarted by the courage and resolution of Fernando Alvarez Pérez, the plane's captain who refused to divert the plane and landed at the international airport in the Cuban capital, the frustrated hijacker, once on land, murdered the pilot and the guard Edor Reyes García and seriously injured co-pilot Evans Rosales. The whole country was shocked by this event.

Other forms of terrorism also persisted.

On October 12, 1971, a speedboat and a larger vessel, coming from U.S. territory, machine-gunned the town of Boca de Sama, on the north coast of Oriente province. This cowardly action against the civilian population resulted in two dead and several other people from the town wounded, including two children.

In those years, terrorism also took the shape of paramilitary actions against merchant vessels and fishing boats from Cuba or third countries in the Straits of Florida. On October 4, 1973, the Cuban fishing boats *Cayo Largo 17* and *Cayo Largo 34* were attacked by two gunboats manned by terrorists, who murdered fisherman Roberto Torna Mirabal and abandoned the others on rubber rafts, without food or water.

Undoubtedly the most atrocious and repulsive act of terrorism perpetrated against Cuba in that period took place on October 6, 1976, when a Cubana Airlines plane with 73 people on board was blown up in mid-flight. Fifty-seven passengers were Cuban, including the 24 members of the junior fencing team who had just won all the gold medals in a Central American championship. Eleven passengers were young people from Guyana, six of whom had chosen to study medicine in Cuba. Also, five passengers were citizens of the Democratic People's Republic of Korea. There were no survivors.

The aircraft, a DC-8 with registration number CUT-1201, had taken off from the international airport in Barbados 10 minutes before. A programmed explosive device had been set off in the plane's toilet by two individuals who, traveling from Trinidad and Tobago, had left the aircraft at that regular stopover on its route. At the airport, they immediately took a taxi and asked the driver to take them to the United States Embassy, according to testimony by Maurice Firebrace, the taxi driver who drove them and gave this deposition to the Barbadian authorities. Another taxi driver, Roger Pilgrim, also testified to the Barbadian authorities that, on the afternoon of that same day, he took both men to the U.S. Embassy on two occasions: first, between 2.00 and 3.00 p.m., and then at around 4:55 p.m. That same afternoon, from the Village Hotel they managed to communicate with, and report to, their bosses in Venezuela that their mission had been accomplished. In the evening, they returned to Trinidad and Tobago, where on October 7, at dawn, they were identified and arrested by the local authorities, to whom they almost immediately confessed their participation in the crimes.

At a meeting held in Trinidad and Tobago, 14 days after the sabotage, at the request of that country's Prime Minister Eric Williams, the foreign minister of Guyana, Fred Willis, referred to the notebooks belonging to the accused which incriminated the CIA by revealing its links with the detainees. They were two mercenaries of Venezuelan nationality who had been hired by Orlando Bosch Avila and Luis Posada Carriles, two of the best-known terrorists recruited by the Central Intelligence Agency since 1960 and experts in sophisticated sabotage techniques with every sort of equipment. Both were registered as members of an organization called CORU [Co-ordination Committee of United Revolutionary Organizations], which emerged from the CIA-ordered unification of the main groups that had until then been acting under different names from U.S. territory. This organization was given the task of carrying out an ambitious program of sabotage and terrorist acts against Cuba, with the full support of the U.S. Government.

About that time, the same group unified by the CIA carried out, among others, the following actions:

The People of Cuba Vs The Government of the USA

- **April 6 [1976]**, two fishing vessels, *Ferro-119* and *Ferro-123*, are attacked by pirate speedboats from Florida, killing fisherman Bienvenido Mauriz and causing great damage to the vessels.
- **April 22**, a bomb set off at the Cuban Embassy in Portugal kills two diplomats, Adriana Corcho Callejas and Efrén Monteagudo Rodríguez and seriously wounds several others, completely destroying the premises.
- **June 5**, the Cuban mission to the UN is the target of an attack with explosives causing major material damage.
- **July 9**, a bomb explodes in the cart carrying the luggage to a Cubana Airlines plane in Kingston airport, Jamaica, a moment before the luggage was transshipped. That is, it was out of sheer luck that a Cubana aircraft was not blown up while in flight that day.
- **July 10**, a bomb explodes in the British West Indies offices in Barbados representing Cubana Airlines in that country.
- **July 23**, a technician from the National Fishing Institute, Artagnán Díaz Díaz, is murdered in the aftermath of an attempt to kidnap the Cuban consul in Mérida.
- **August 9**, two staff members of the Cuban Embassy in Argentina, Crescencio Galañena Hernández and Jesús Cejas Arias, are kidnapped and they have never been heard of again.
- **August 18**, a bomb explodes in the Cubana Airlines offices in Panama, causing considerable damage.

The groups that made up the CORU had been issuing public statements in the United States, claiming responsibility for each of these misdeeds. In August 1976, a Miami newspaper published a shameless war report where, after relating how they had blown up a motor car opposite the Cuban Embassy in Colombia and destroyed the offices of Air Panama, the CORU ringleaders concluded: "We will very soon attack aircraft in flight." Approximately six weeks later, the Cuban aircraft that made a stopover in Barbados exploded in mid-flight.

Orlando Bosch and Luis Posada Carriles were arrested, jailed and subjected to a long, complicated legal process in Venezuela together with the two Venezuelan mercenaries who — following their orders — had set off the bomb in the Cubana Airlines DC-8 aircraft. In August 1985, Posada Carriles was rescued by the CIA through the so-called Cuban American National Foundation [CANF] from San Juan de los Moros maximum security prison and taken in a matter of hours to El Salvador, where he was immediately put to work in one of the most secret, delicate and incriminating operations undertaken by a U.S. administration: the notorious Iran-Contra operation, which led to a huge political scandal in the United States. Posada Carriles was in charge of storing and, in practice, distributing the weapons for the dirty war in Nicaragua, under direct orders from the White House. He had never had such senior responsibilities in his 25 years of service to the U.S. Government.

Orlando Bosch, who had been at the head of the operation in the loathsome crime because he was then higher-ranking than Posada Carriles in the terrorist organization unified by the CIA, was cynically acquitted by a corrupt and shameless court. The perpetrator of numerous acts of terrorism against Cuba now lives peacefully as a distinguished guest of the United States of America.

Another shameful and painful terrorist action was committed after the brutal crime in Barbados: on September 11, 1980, Cuban diplomat Félix García Rodríguez was murdered in a crowded New York street in broad daylight. The crime was perpetrated by a commando from the terrorist organization known as Omega-7, whose task was to assassinate this diplomat and three other officials from the Cuban mission to the United Nations.

The changes in the international arena have led to changes in the expression of what is nothing but flagrant state terrorism against the Republic of Cuba. By this token, the most reactionary sectors of Cuban immigrants in the United States encouraged terrorist activities during the last period of Republican President George Bush's administration — which marked the development of somewhat significant actions under the first and second administrations of Democrat President William Clinton.

From 1992 until the present, the Cuban American National Foundation, a prominent financial contributor to presidential political campaigns and to a group of well-known American legislators, has planned, organized and financed with impunity in the United States this terrorist campaign against Cuba. This was clearly demonstrated during the recent trials against terrorists Raúl Ernesto Cruz León and Otto René Rodríguez Llerena, who exploded seven bombs in Havana hotels in 1997. The CANF has carried out its actions not only from U.S. territory itself, using mercenaries of Cuban origin who are residents in the United States, but also from Central America, recruiting Central American mercenaries acting under the orders of notorious terrorist Luis Posada Carriles.

These recent criminal actions against Cuba originated in Central America — planned, organized and financed by the leaders of a Cuban American Mafia in the United States — were unquestionably carried out with the acquiescence and tolerance of the American authorities, for whom Posada Carriles always worked and who have never severed relations with him.

In addition, and as part of its political strategy, the U.S. Government has for 40 years given major encouragement to the illegal emigration toward its territory, not only as an instrument in the ideological struggle and in its campaigns to discredit Cuba, but also to promote indiscipline and social unrest. That has resulted in criminal acts because criminals were convinced that they would be welcomed and protected in the United States once they had achieved the main goal of departing from Cuba. This has not been the case with citizens from other parts of the world who tried to emigrate to the United States without first obtaining a visa.

This cynical policy has been the source of many incidents, but January 9, 1992, was a milestone. On that day, Revolutionary National Police officers Yuri Gómez Rivero and Rolando Pérez Quintosa were murdered along with Coastguard member Orosmán Dueñas Valero and civilian security guard Rafael Guevara Borges, a worker at the "José Martí" Children's Camp in Havana. They were assaulted and murdered by a group of criminals — led by Luis Miguel Almeida Pérez — who intended to hijack a boat for leaving the country illegally.

Likewise, on August 4, 1994, Revolutionary National Police officer Gabriel Lamouth Caballero was murdered by anti-social elements trying to leave the country illegally through the port of Havana and, on August 8, 1994, Lieutenant Roberto Aguilar Reyes was killed when an auxiliary ship of the Revolutionary Navy was hijacked in Mariel, Havana, by Leonel Macías González, who managed to flee to the United States where he was welcomed as a hero and has enjoyed complete impunity after his cowardly act of murder.

As a result of the terrorist activities promoted by the U.S. Government against our country throughout four decades — from the triumph of the [1959] Revolution until today — 234 innocent people have lost their lives or been incapacitated. Evidence of this is provided in the documents attached to this Claim marked with the numbers 14, 15, 16, 17, 18 and 19.

To have an idea of the intensity reached by terrorist activity against Cuba at a given moment, suffice it to say that in only 14 months, from November 30, 1961 — the day President Kennedy approved the implementation of the so-called Cuba Project — up to the month of January 1963, a total of 5,780 acts of terrorism were perpetrated against Cuba, 716 of which can be described as substantial sabotage of industrial facilities.

The complete lack of scruples on the part of the United States, along with its immorality and inability to abide by civilized standards of political practice is best expressed in the plans conceived by that country's leadership for the physical elimination of the leader of the Cuban Revolution, initially in his capacity as Prime Minister from February 16, 1959, to December 3, 1976, and later as head of state.

On December 11, 1959, Colonel J.C. King, head of the CIA Western Hemisphere Division, in a secret memorandum to CIA Director Allen Dulles recommended that: "Thorough consideration be given to the elimination of Fidel Castro. None of those close to Fidel, such as his brother Raúl or his companion Che Guevara, have the same mesmeric appeal to the masses. Many informed people believe that the disappearance of Fidel would greatly accelerate the fall of the present Government."

From that date up to the present, Cuban State Security has disclosed, investigated, uncovered or neutralized 637 attempts on the life of Commander-in-Chief Fidel Castro, of which there were plausible indications of meticulously conceived or drawn-up plans. The plans were in an advanced stage of organization and implementation or about to be implemented, and include those not implemented due to the cowardice of some who even managed to get within a few meters of their target. One can only guess at how many other plans have never been known.

The U.S. Senate has investigated and verified at least eight such conspiracies, that is, barely 1.25 percent of those directly organized by the CIA or induced by the hostility, propaganda, conspiratorial tolerance and actions of the U.S. Government against Cuba — a campaign which has already lasted for 40 years.

GUANTÁNAMO NAVAL BASE

SIXTH: The Guantánamo Naval Base has been used by the United States as an instrument of its aggressive policy against our country. The Guantánamo Naval Base was set up in Cuba almost a hundred years ago following a confusing and treacherously drafted agreement by virtue of which the United States leased the territory occupied by the base "for the time required," without a clause safeguarding our full right to sovereignty over the said territory.

After the triumph of the Revolution, U.S. military authorities and special agencies immediately offered protection in this enclave to nearly a thousand murderers and henchmen of Batista's regime.

The base was turned into an active center of subversion and provocation against our country.

Numerous mercenaries and fugitives from Cuban justice for their crimes and misdeeds have found sanctuary and impunity there.

Numerous people, encouraged by the privilege of entering the United States without a visa, chose to leave the country illegally through that military facility, which is maintained in Cuba by force.

It has been common practice since the triumph of the Revolution for this base to be used as a safe haven for despicable traitors who went there in hijacked aircraft and boats, and in no case have these criminals been extradited.

Article 2 of the aforementioned Agreement [on Guantánamo], signed on February 16, 1903, gave the United States a certain right, under certain conditions that it accepted and committed itself to honor, "[...] to do any and all things necessary to fit the premises for use as coaling or naval stations only, and for no other purpose."

Article 4 of the Supplementary Agreement of July 2, 1903, also signed by the governments of Cuba and the United States, set forth in precise and clear terms that: "Fugitives from justice charged with crimes or misdemeanors amenable to Cuban law, taking refuge within said areas, shall be delivered up by the United States authorities on demand by duly authorized Cuban authorities."

It is unjustifiable that a costly military base — kept at the expense of the U.S. budget and taxpayers despite its being absolutely useless to the national security of the United States —

should occupy a valuable part of our territory just to humiliate, harass and attack the Cuban people, its sole mission in the past decades.

It has been particularly arbitrary and abusive to keep that military enclave against the will of our people after the end of the Cold War, especially when the U.S. Government is dismantling dozens of facilities on its territory and abroad to reduce its military budget. Ninety six years after that commitment was entered by both parties under Article 1 of the February 1903 Agreement — signed by the U.S. Government and a weak and compliant [Cuban] government lacking foresight which leased the land to the United States "for the time required" — it is evident that the United States has not needed such land for a long time now for anything other than its aggressive policy against Cuba, a right not included even in that ominous agreement. It is not just that one of Cuba's best bays is used for that purpose.

Between 1962 and 1994 — the year both governments, on their own initiative, agreed to take measures to reduce the risks of incidents, after the migratory agreement had been signed by Cuba and the United States of America — a total of 13,498 acts of provocation originated from the base. The most common of these included offensive language, obscene gestures and pornographic scenes, violations of the dividing line by breaking parts of the fence and, in other cases, by crossing the line into free territory; the illumination of the Cuban soldiers' sentry boxes with searchlights, the use of firearms, the threatening pointing of guns, tanks and machine-guns against Cuban staff and facilities; repeated violations of Cuban airspace, including the landing of helicopters outside the base perimeter, as well as violations of our territorial waters.

The Cuban revolutionary government has presented numerous official notes to the U.S. Government protesting these incidents but, in the vast majority of cases, there has not been a reply that is in accordance with international law. Cuba has also made multiple denunciations in international agencies and many foreign journalists have visited the border perimeter, interviewed witnesses, learned of and obtained evidence about the denounced violations. For more than 30 years, Cuba has submitted evidence of such acts of aggression and not one U.S. administration has ever apologized. On the other hand, the United States cannot show a single case of a

The People of Cuba Vs The Government of the USA

Cuban provocation, violation or penetration in the territory arbitrarily occupied by its troops.

Cuban soldiers of the Border Patrol and citizens of our country have been killed or wounded from the territory of the base or in the base itself, namely:

- In January 5, 1961, worker Manuel Prieto Gómez, who was one of the few Cubans to keep his job there and who had worked in that facility for 13 years, was savagely tortured at the Guantánamo Naval Base.
- In September 30, 1961, [U.S.] Marine Captain Arthur J. Jackson arrested another Cuban — Rubén López Sabariego — who was working there as a freight truck driver. Fifteen days after his arrest, the chargé d'affaires of the Swiss embassy in Cuba reported that a dead body had been found in a ditch inside the military facility. The autopsy showed that the man had been dead for several days and had broken bones and bruises caused by torture.
- In May 1962, Rodolfo Rosell Salas was kidnapped by naval base staff while he was working as a fisherman. He was murdered and his corpse was found on July 14.
- In July 18, 1964, Border Battalion soldier Ramón López Peña was killed by shots fired from the base by an American soldier on guard duty in the position situated at co-ordinates 43-67.
- In May 21, 1966, Private Luis Ramírez López was also murdered by shots fired by American soldiers from the Guantánamo Naval Base.

As a result of aggressions originating from the Naval Base, a total of eight Cubans have died and 15 others have been left incapacitated. This is accredited with the corresponding certificates in annexed documents marked with the numbers 20 and 21.

In addition, great injustices were committed against the thousands of Cubans who worked in the Naval Base.

In January 1964, over 3,000 Cubans worked in that base, of which approximately 2,300 were admitted to enter and leave the base every day.

Between February 10 and 15, 1964, all 500 of said workers were fired on orders from the U.S. Government. Between February and

October 1,060 others were also fired, making a total of 1,560 — two-thirds [of the workforce] in only seven months — and so it continued until less than 100 workers were allowed to keep their jobs there.

Another cruel measure: on March 5, 1966, the U.S. Defense Department announced that the policy of its government "would not allow the payment of pensions to any personnel in Cuba," therefore, those who had been fired could neither receive a pension nor claim the return of their contributions to the pensioners' fund held by the U.S. Government. Thus, the Cuban workers in that base were left with the choice of applying for asylum or losing their jobs and every other right therein.

Presently, there remain only 17 Cuban workers at the base who are admitted every day to that facility.

BIOLOGICAL WARFARE

SEVENTH: That, in all these years of Revolution, the U.S. Government's acts of aggression have had a significant impact on our people's health. This criminal policy has been aimed at obstructing and hindering the impressive achievements that Cuban social policy has won. For this purpose, the United States has used, among other things, biological warfare which has cost precious human lives, including children and pregnant women.

On May 1981, at the Boyeros municipality in the Cuban capital, reports began of people sick with fever, ocular, abdominal and muscular pains, rashes, cephalalgia and asthenia frequently accompanied by multiple bleeding with different degrees of severity. A few days later, there was an outbreak of similar cases in the provinces of Cienfuegos, Holguín and Villa Clara, by then rapidly extending to the rest of the country.

The initial studies demonstrated that the first cases had appeared simultaneously in three places on the island at a distance of more than 300 kilometers one from the other. There was no epidemiological explanation that would allow us to interpret these incidents as a natural infection.

Laboratory studies confirmed that the etiological agent was the dengue type 2 virus. The fact that the virus showed up unexpectedly, when no dengue-2 epidemic activity had been reported in the American continent or in any country with which Cuba had a significant exchange of personnel, as well as its simultaneous appearance in different regions of the country, are elements that substantiate the studies carried out by prestigious Cuban scientists, with the cooperation of foreign scientists highly specialized in detecting and fighting biological warfare.

The exhaustive research and studies carried out led to the conclusion that the epidemic was deliberately introduced in the national territory by agents at the service of the U.S. Government. American experts in biological warfare had been the only ones who had obtained a variety of the *Aedes aegypti* mosquito, very much associated with the transmission of the type-2 dengue virus, according to a statement by Colonel Phillip Russell at the 14th International Congress on the Pacific Ocean, held in 1979, only two years before the outbreak of the brutal epidemic in Cuba.

It is significant that in 1975, American scientist Charles Henry Calisher, on a visit to Cuba, took an interest in and obtained information on the existence of antibodies to dengue in the Cuban population and the non-existence in the population, for at least 45 years, of antibodies for the type-2 dengue virus.

In the trial held in the United States in 1984 against Eduardo Arocena, a ringleader of the terrorist organization Omega-7, he publicly confessed to having introduced germs into Cuba and admitted that hemorrhagic dengue fever had been introduced in the island by U.S.-based groups of Cuban origin.

Whether or not the confession made by the leader of the well-known terrorist organization Omega-7 about the groups used to introduce hemorrhagic dengue fever in Cuba is true, we have exhaustively explained and demonstrated here who those groups were, who organized them and in whose service they were acting.

Furthermore, the U.S. army had reported the existence of a vaccine that included protection against dengue-2 which was applied to the population inside Guantánamo Naval Base. Of course, not a single case of the disease was recorded in that military enclave while the epidemic hit the rest of the island's territory without exception.

From November 18 to 20 and on December 2, 9, 18 and 19, 1969, during the 91st U.S. Congress, a hearing was held to analyze alleged plans concerning the use of biological warfare against Cuba.

The following dialogue took place in that session:

"Mr. Fraser: It has been said the United States was prepared to use biological agents with regard to the invasion of Cuba. Can you tell us whether that is true?

"Mr. Pickering: I just have no knowledge of that.

"Mr. Fraser: Has anyone here any information on that question? (No response.)

"Mr. Pickering: I have seen the discussions of this subject in the press.

"Mr. McCarthy: I would say the Senate Foreign Relations Committee is familiar with the incidents alluded to and there are people in the Government who know what the record is, present and past. I know the information is available in your records."

The use of insects to transmit diseases has been carefully studied in Fort Detrick. A journalist reported that the insect inventory at Fort Detrick in 1959 included mosquitoes infected with yellow fever, malaria and dengue; fleas infected with plague; ticks with tularemia, relapsing fever and Colorado fever; and houseflies infected with cholera, anthrax and dysentery.

According to data released by the U.S. Army some 20 years ago, in July 1958 the Center for Bacteriological Weapons of the U.S. Ground Forces conducted experiments with *Aedes aegypti* mosquitoes which carried yellow fever. These experiments were carried out on a landing field in the state of Florida. The swarm of mosquitoes — not infected, of course — and made up of approximately 600,000 specimens was dispersed over the landing field from a plane. The results of the research showed that, in one day, the mosquitoes could reach distances of 1.6 to 3.2 kilometers and bit many people and that the *Aedes aegypti* had great potential to carry yellow fever over long distances.

On October 29, 1980, a press dispatch from Washington reported that:

"...The U.S. Government seriously considered using yellow-fever mosquitoes against the Soviet Union in 1956.

"Declassified military documents released today state that the U.S. Army considered using *Aedes aegypti* mosquitoes to spread yellow fever inside the Soviet Union...

"At Fort Detrick, Maryland, experiments are being carried out with millions of yellow-fever mosquitoes. These laboratories can produce half a million mosquitoes every month, and work on a new plant designed by the Army, with a capacity for 130 million mosquitoes a month, is about to begin...

"The declassified documents assert that the possible aggression against the Soviet Union is based on the Soviet Union's inability to implement a program of massive immunization against such a mosquito attack."

This was the case with a great power [the Soviet Union], located at a great distance and in a vast territory, with which the United States was not at war. However, it clearly toyed with the idea of silent biological sabotage.

The following may serve as a background to explain what happened in Cuba. *The Miami Herald* newspaper, which cannot be suspected of being friendly toward Cuba, published on September 1, 1981, an article which read:

"WASHINGTON. The pompous statement by Fidel Castro that the 'harmful plagues' that are destroying crops and animals in Cuba and the dengue fever epidemic that has brought about the death of over 100 people in the island are the doings of the Central Intelligence Agency (CIA) does not seem inconceivable to the authors of a new book that shall be put out this autumn.

"William W. Turner, former agent of the Federal Bureau of Investigations, and journalist Warren Hinckle, state that the United States used biological warfare against Cuba during the Nixon administration.

"The authors argue that the CIA has committed the United States to a secret, undeclared and illegal war against Cuba for more than 20 years. The so-called Cuba Project is the largest and least known operated by the CIA outside the legal limits of its statutes, they say.

"The history of the Cuba Project is the history of an important U.S. war not declared by Congress, not acknowledged by Washington, and not reported in the press."

Before that, a UPI cable dated in Washington on January 9, 1977, reported the following:

> "*Newsday*, a Long Island (New York) newspaper, said that at least with the tacit support of the CIA, agents related to anti-Castro terrorists introduced the African swine fever virus in Cuba in 1971.
>
> "Six weeks later, an outbreak of the disease forced Cuban health authorities to sacrifice 500,000 pigs in order to avoid an animal epidemic of national proportions.
>
> "An unidentified source of the CIA revealed to *Newsday* that at the beginning of 1971 he was given a container with virus at Fort Gulick, a U.S. Army base situated in the Panama Canal Zone also used by the CIA, and that the container had been taken on a fishing boat by underground agents in Cuba.
>
> "It was the first time the disease appeared in the Western Hemisphere.
>
> "It is known, through their own admission, that when the African swine fever broke out in Cuba, the CIA and the U.S. Army were experimenting with poisons, deadly toxins, products to destroy crops and other techniques of bacteriological warfare."

There is a mountain of evidence, background information and facts that cannot possibly be ignored.

What is beyond question is that, in just a few weeks, the hemorrhagic dengue epidemic in Cuba — where it had never existed — had affected a total of 344,203 people, a figure with no known precedent in any other country of the world. Another record was set when 11,400 new patients were reported in a single day on July 6, 1981.

A total of 116,143 cases were hospitalized. About 24,000 patients suffered from hemorrhaging and 10,224 suffered some degree of dengue-induced shock.

One hundred and fifty-eight people died as a result of the epidemic, including 101 children.

The whole country and all its resources were mobilized to fight the epidemic. The vector's presence was strongly and simultaneously controlled in every Cuban town and city, using all possible means and with products and equipment urgently bought from anywhere, including the United States. A request was made to the United States through the Pan-American Health Organization and finally, in the month of August, an important larvicide could be bought. Chemicals and equipment were brought in, often by plane and sometimes from countries as far away as Japan, whose factories sold Cuba thousands of individual motor fumigators. Malathion had to be brought from Europe at a transportation fee of $5,000 a ton, that is, three and a half times the cost of the product.

In addition to the existing hospital network, dozens of boarding schools were turned into hospitals in order to isolate every new patient reported, without exception. At the same time, intensive-care units were built and equipped in all of the country's children's hospitals.

The last infected case was reported on October 10, 1981.

If it had not been for this enormous effort, tens of thousands of people, the vast majority of them children, would have died. An epidemic that many experts had forecast would take years to eradicate was defeated in little more than four months. The adverse economic impact was also considerable.

The list of the dead as a result of the epidemic is authenticated through the corresponding certifications issued by the Ministry of Public Health, and attached as document number 22.

DIRECT MILITARY AGGRESSION

EIGHTH: That, throughout the Cuban revolutionary process — a strictly internal affair which our people carried out exercising their right to full sovereignty as citizens of an independent nation — our homeland has had to face, and still does, the constant danger of a direct military aggression from the United States.

One of the first meetings of the Cuba Project task force, reported in a memorandum drafted by the CIA director on January 19, 1962, was especially significant. The meeting was held exactly nine months after the crushing defeat on April 19, 1961 — after less than 72 hours — and the capture of the entire expeditionary force that landed at the Bay of Pigs, within sight of the U.S. fleet standing by some three miles off the coast.

The fleet's presence and encouragement was of no use to the mercenary troops. It did not even have time to act and there was nobody to rescue when, by the end of the adventure, President Kennedy had been persuaded to give the invaders air cover by using the fighter planes on board the *Essex* aircraft-carrier, which was in the naval detachment. According to a declassified document on the meeting that took place on January 19, 1962, Robert Kennedy, the U.S. attorney general, said to those in attendance that the President considered that the last chapter on Cuba had yet to be written, that Castro's overthrow was possible and that carrying out that objective was of utmost priority. The document stated: "The solution to the Cuban problem today carries the top priority in the United States Government. All else is secondary."

On March 7, 1962, the Joint Chiefs of Staff stated in a secret document: "...determination that a credible internal revolt is impossible to attain during the next 9-10 months will require a decision by the United States to develop a Cuban 'provocation' as justification for positive U.S. military action."

On March 9, 1962, under the title "Pretexts to Justify U.S. Military Intervention in Cuba," the Office of the Secretary of Defense submitted to the Joint Chiefs of Staff a package of harassment measures aimed at creating conditions to justify a military intervention in Cuba. The measures considered included the following:

- "A series of well coordinated incidents will be planned to take place in and around Guantánamo [Naval Base] to give a genuine appearance of being carried out by hostile Cuban forces."
- "The United States would respond by executing offensive operations to secure water and power supplies, destroying artillery and mortar emplacements threatening the base. Commence large-scale United States military operations.
- "A 'Remember the Maine' incident could be arranged in several forms:
  - "We could blow up a U.S. ship in Guantánamo Bay and blame Cuba.
  - "We could blow up a drone (unmanned) vessel anywhere in the Cuban waters.
  - "We could arrange to cause such incident in the vicinity of Havana or Santiago as a spectacular result of a Cuban attack from the air or sea, or both.
  - "The presence of Cuban planes or ships merely investigating the intent of the vessel could be fairly

compelling evidence that the ship was taken under attack.
- "The U.S. could follow up with an air/sea rescue operation covered by U.S. fighters to 'evacuate' remaining members of the non-existent crew.
- "Casualty lists in U.S. newspapers would cause a helpful wave of national indignation.
- "We could develop a Communist-Cuban terror campaign in the Miami area, in other Florida cities and even in Washington. The terror campaign could be pointed at Cuban refugees seeking haven in the United States.
- "We could sink a boatload of Cubans en route to Florida (real or simulated).
- "We could foster attempts on lives of Cuban refugees in the United States, even to the extent of wounding, in instances to be widely publicized.
- "Exploding a few plastic bombs in carefully chosen spots, the arrest of Cuban agents and the release of prepared documents substantiating Cuban involvement would also be helpful in projecting the idea of an irresponsible government.
- "A 'Cuban-based, Castro-supported' filibuster could be simulated against a neighboring Caribbean nation.
- "Use of MIG-type aircraft by U.S. pilots could provide additional provocation.
- "Harassment of civil aircraft, attacks on surface shipping and destruction of U.S. military drone aircraft by MIG-type planes would be useful as complementary actions.
- "An F-86 properly painted would convince air passengers that they saw a Cuban MIG, especially if the pilot of the transport were to announce such fact.
- "Hijacking attempts against civil air and surface craft should appear to continue as harassing measures condoned by the government of Cuba.
- "It is possible to create an incident which will demonstrate convincingly that a Cuban aircraft has attacked and shot down a chartered civil airliner en route from the United States to Jamaica, Guatemala, Panama or Venezuela.

- "The passengers could be a group of college students off on a holiday or any grouping of persons with a common interest to support chartering a non-scheduled flight.
- "It is possible to create an incident which will make it appear that Communist-Cuban MIGs have destroyed a U.S.A.F. aircraft over international waters in an unprovoked attack."

Five months later, in August 1962, General Maxwell D. Taylor, chairman of the Joint Chiefs of Staff, confirmed to President Kennedy that no possibility was perceived whereby the Cuban Government could be overthrown without direct U.S. military intervention, which was why the Special Group-Augmented was recommending the even more aggressive approach of Operation Mongoose. Kennedy authorized its implementation as "a matter of urgency."

These plans to invade Cuba, which were hatched in early 1962, and of which highly plausible news reached the governments of the Soviet Union and Cuba, determined the coordinated decision by both countries to urgently install the strategic missiles whose presence gave rise to the October [1962 Missile] Crisis that same year.

Today, in view of the confessed and proven facts, nobody would have any right to doubt who — in their obsession against the Cuban Revolution — was responsible for the world having been on the verge of a thermonuclear war.

BURDEN OF DEFENSE ALERT

NINTH: The undeniable reality, proven by facts and documents that nobody would dare challenge, explains the huge expenditures in economic and human resources and the sacrifices imposed on our people over 40 years to defend themselves from the danger of a direct armed aggression by the United States of America.

Cuba's defense needs do not compare with those of any other country in the world. This imposed the unavoidably inordinate scale of the people's preparation to ensure their own survival.

The basic idea has been to prevent war by maintaining and developing an armed-response potential involving all the people and a doctrine of struggle against a military invasion that would extract such a high price from the invaders as would discourage a direct aggression from the United States. For a long time, this activity has required, and received, top priority.

In the past few years, it has been possible to reduce the regular troops thanks precisely to that concept, despite the marked increase in the hostility against Cuba in the past few decades. Notwithstanding the significant savings that this has meant, defense continues to be the country's main priority. The effort put into training millions of men and women every year and the maintenance of the people's fighting status, the construction of expensive shelters and other fortifications to protect the civilian population and combatants — on which greater emphasis had to be put due to the rapid technological development achieved by the United States in the military field — have required and continue to require considerable investment in human and material resources.

According to estimates, in the period from 1960 to 1998, we were forced into over-manning in terms of the number of defense-related personnel. Internationally accepted parameters set out that a country's defense force should amount to around 0.4 percent of its population. Following this criterion, our country has been forced to go considerably beyond these parameters, as a result of the war situation imposed on us all these years. This imbalance in terms of personnel is estimated at about 4,362,645 mobilized troops, during that period, exceeding the internationally accepted parameters.

The situation described — an absolute anomaly for a small country of limited economic resources and a low demographic rate — and the standing threat posed by the mightiest military power in the world, resulted in an enormous and extraordinary effort in the training of a fighting force made necessary by the U.S. policy of aggression — a policy which resulted in the loss of 2,354 human lives and the disability of 1,833 people. These elements are properly documented in annexes 23 and 24.

The events hereby exposed have proven beyond doubt the civil liability of the government of the United States of America in the war that for 40 years it has conducted against our nation, its institutions and organizations.

Such extreme actions have forced the social and mass organizations that we represent in this process to wage an intense battle in every front, in the light of the multifaceted aggressions carried out by a superpower. The United States has turned the so-called "Cuban issue" into a matter of domestic politics, the target of manipulation, scheming, deceitful posturing and personal and partisan ambitions. The U.S. Congress adopts legislation of a marked extraterritorial and interfering nature — whilst enacting regulations intended for acceptance by Cuba and the rest of the world — to support its intent to dominate our country.

Although these elements are not the factual grounds of our Claim, they have been recounted so that this Court can make a comprehensive evaluation of the scope of the damages described herein and, consequently, of the size of the requested compensation.

That, the present Claim is based on the following:

LEGAL GROUNDS

1. That, this Claim is instituted through Ordinary Proceeding bearing in mind that the amount claimed as reparation and compensation for damages exceeds that which is stipulated in Article 223.1 of the Law of Civil, Administrative and Labor Proceeding.
2. That, this Claim falls under the jurisdiction of the Havana City Provincial People's Court by reason of its subject matter and because its economic content exceeds what is prescribed in Article 6.1 of the Law of Civil, Administrative and Labor Proceeding. Also, that this court is relevant by reason of its location and our implicit subordination to it, supported by Article 10.1, as it relates to Article 8, both from the aforesaid Procedural Law.
3. That, this Claim we are filing has been structured in compliance with the corresponding requisites set forth in Article 224, with the supporting documents proving the rationale for our testimony accompanying the trial brief as stipulated in Article 226, as well as the documents where we explain the rights we are pleading pursuant to provisions in Article 227. That, the corresponding copies are attached in order to proceed to subpoena the defendant according to Article 228; all these articles are contained in the Law of Civil, Administrative and Labor Proceeding.
4. That, by virtue of this Claim, the defendant shall be subpoenaed through a Rogatory Commission, a procedure to be effected through the Ministry of Foreign Affairs of the

Republic of Cuba in compliance with provisions in Article 229 and 230, related to Article 170, all of them contained in the Law of Civil Procedure.

5. That, in accordance with the concrete claim of this lawsuit, the ruling pronounced in due course shall be consistent with the petition of penalty, as supported by Article 146 of the above mentioned Procedural Law.

6. That, those people whose names have been listed in the introduction to this Claim are legitimately entitled to promote this process in their capacity as president, national coordinator or secretary general, as appropriate, on behalf of the legal entities they represent since they hold senior positions in said organizations which represent the specific interests of their membership as stipulated in those organizations' own rules, all this pursuant to provisions in Articles 39.1 and 2.c, 40, 41 and 42 of the Civil Code, as they relate to Article 64 of the Law of Civil, Administrative and Labor Proceeding and Article 7 of the Constitution of the Republic of Cuba.

7. That, the present Claim is based on the violation of the civil rights of Cuban citizens, particularly the right to life and the right to physical integrity, acknowledged as rights inherent to the human person in Article 38 of the Civil Code, whose violation legitimizes a claim of reparation and compensation for damages caused, as prescribed in Section c) of the above mentioned Civil Code.

8. That, the concrete claim derived from this lawsuit is supported by subsection d) in Article 111 of the Civil Code, in as much as the breach of the said civil rights presupposes the non-contractual liability of the defendant, in its capacity as debtor, with regards to the obligation to compensate and make amends for the damages caused, as prescribed in the general principle of law known as *neminem laedere*, which is imputed as violated.

9. That, the illegal action attributed to the debtor, in its capacity as defendant, entails causing damages to another and it is, at the same time, the source of a civil juridical relation and, more precisely, of an obligatory juridical relation whose content presupposes the release of benefits to compensate the author, a responsibility that in the light of Cuban civil law is markedly objective as sustained in Article 81, related to Article 47, subsection c), 46, Section 3, and 82 of the Civil Code.

10. That, the content of the compensation for the civil liability includes, among others, reparation for material damages in payment for the value of the goods and that being, this time, goods of incalculable value and irreplaceable due to their very nature — such as human life and physical integrity — a financial valuation and compensation is warranted in the amount requested in the principal of this Claim as prescribed in Article 83, subsection b), related to Article 85, both in the Civil Code and reparation for the moral damages through public recanting by the offender, as established in Article 88 of the same legislation.

    Likewise, the compensation would include reparation for damages caused in cases of death or disability, expanded to include the costs of sustaining the family, an obligation that until now has been assumed by the Cuban society. Also, all earnings which they failed to receive due to the absence of that family member and what it represents for the disabled in terms of the loss, or decrease, of their wages and the impossibility to fully reassume their social life due to physical deformities or sequels and thus their inability to work, as well as all the expenses that the victims or their families had to incur in order to restore the physical and mental health of the injured, as provided in Article 86, subsections a), b), d) and e), as they relate to Article 87, subsection c) of the Civil Code.

11. That, because they took place inside the national territory of the Republic of Cuba, or in diplomatic missions, maritime vessels and aircraft registered in Cuba, or against people working abroad, or other cases with similar rights to protection, the law that applies is the Cuban national law, as prescribed in Article 16 of the Civil Code.

12. That, the previously mentioned juridical rules covering the substantive order of the present Claim should be interpreted and applied in accordance with the political, social and economic foundations of the Cuban state as expressed in Chapter 1 of the Constitution of the Republic of Cuba and prescribed in Article 2 of the Civil Code.

13. That, the aforesaid rules of the Civil Code presently in force are applicable to the full content of the present Claim since the obligatory juridical relations established under the previous legislation are still valid in as much as their effects, subsequent

to the enforcement of the present Civil Code, are governed by their provisions, as stipulated by the Civil Code First Transitory Provision.
14. That, the representation of the signing attorneys is based on that which is prescribed in Article 414 of the Civil Code.

CONCRETE CLAIM

That, pursuant to the concept of *reparation for material damages*, the Court would rule that the defendant, as a debtor with civil liability, is ordered to pay for the lives of the 3,478 people, it being impossible to replace them and their value being incalculable, at a rate equal an average of $30 million for each dead person, which amounts to a total of $104.34 billion, and that it shall pay for the value of the illegally impaired physical integrity of 2,099 people, also irreplaceable *in integrum*, at a rate equal an average of $15 million for each incapacitated person, amounting to a total of $31.485 billion.

That, pursuant to the concept of *compensation for damages*, as reparation for the fringe benefits that the Cuban society has had to assume, as well as other earnings the victims and relatives have failed to receive due to the events related *ut supra*, it is ordered to pay $34.78 billion, equal to an average $10 million for every one of the deceased, and $10.495 billion, equal to $5 million for every incapacitated person.

In accordance with the aforesaid, a ruling is requested as would demand only one payment for the sum of $181.1 billion.

Likewise, it is requested that, pursuant to our Statutory Law the defendant is urged to publicly recant for the moral damages caused to both the relatives and the victims of the events exposed in this claim.

That, the Claim we are submitting for the value of the lives of 3,478 dead Cubans and 2,099 incapacitated Cubans is substantially less than the amount fixed by Mr. Lawrence King, Civil Judge in Florida's South District, who in the trials number 96-10126, 96-10127 and 96-10128 sentenced the Republic of Cuba to pay $187,627,911 for the death of pilots Armando Alejandre, Carlos Alberto Costa and Mario M. De la Pena in the incident provoked by the countless violations of the Cuban air space repeated for years, thus demanding an average of $62,542,637 for each dead man. Such figure derives from the summation of a compensation for two concepts: *compensatory damages* and *punitive damages*, in compliance with their laws, which can be compared with the average $40 million for each dead person that the Cuban people claim, also based on two concepts: *reparation for material damages* and *compensation for damages*, in compliance with our laws.

Had we resorted to the same basis for calculation as were used by Judge Lawrence King, our Claim would amount to $217.523 billion, that is, $78.403 billion in excess of our present claim.

THEREFORE

WE REQUEST FROM THE COURT: To accept this complaint as duly submitted, accompanied by its copies and the documents justifying the representation and the right we invoke, and consequently to consider as instituted this Claim in Ordinary Proceeding on Compensation for Damages. Also, to consider the *Government of the United States of America* as the defendant and to have it subpoenaed within the legally established time-limit through a Rogatory Commission, for it to appear and respond to what it considers pertinent and, after the realization of the other proceedings, to pronounce its ruling in due course announcing that this Claim stands accepted and issuing a sentence in the manner requested in our Claim.

IN ADDITION: We appeal to this Court so that, pursuant to provisions in Article 170 of the Law of Civil, Administrative and Labor Proceeding, instructions are given to the Ministry of Foreign Affairs of the Republic of Cuba to proceed to subpoena the defendant.

Havana City, May 31, 1999

Juan Mendoza Díaz, Attorney
Leonardo B. Pérez Gallardo, Attorney
Magaly Iserne Carrillo, Attorney
Ivonne Pérez Gutiérrez, Attorney

BOOKS ON CUBA AND THE UNITED STATES

THE BAY OF PIGS AND THE CIA
by Juan Carlos Rodríguez
For the first time, key Cuban files on the Bay of Pigs are published in this new and dramatic interpretation of the first foreign policy debacle that confronted the Kennedy Administration. No CIA document on the Bay of Pigs can be read in the same way after the publication of this Cuban account of the invasion and its aftermath.
ISBN 1-875284-98-2

CIA TARGETS FIDEL
The Secret Assassination Report
Only recently declassified and published for the first time, this secret report was prepared for the CIA on its own plots to assassinate Cuba's Fidel Castro. Under pressure in 1967 when the press were probing the alliance with the Mafia in these murderous schemes, the CIA produced this remarkably frank, single-copy report stamped "secret — eyes only."
ISBN 1-875284-90-7

ZR RIFLE
The Plot to Kill Kennedy and Castro
by Claudia Furiati
Thirty years after the death of President Kennedy, Cuba has opened its secret files on the assassination, showing how and why the CIA, along with anti-Castro exiles and the Mafia, planned the conspiracy.
ISBN 1-875284-85-0

IN THE EYE OF THE STORM
Castro, Khrushchev, Kennedy and the Missile Crisis
by Carlos Lechuga
For the first time, Cuba's view of the most serious crisis of the Cold War is told by one of the leading participants, Cuba's UN ambassador.
ISBN 1-875284-87-7

GUANTANAMO
Bay of Discord: The Story of the U.S. Military Base in Cuba
by Roger Ricardo
This book provides a detailed history of the U.S. base on Cuban soil that has remained from the beginning of the century to the present day. It documents how the base has been used for violations of Cuban territory and why it remains a sticking point in U.S.–Cuba relations.
ISBN 1-875284-56-7

BOOKS ON *CUBA AND THE UNITED STATES*

CUBA AND THE UNITED STATES
A Chronological History
by Jane Franklin
Based on exceptionally wide research, this updated and expanded chronology by U.S. historian Jane Franklin relates day by day, year by year, the developments involving the two neighboring countries from the 1959 Cuban revolution through 1995.
ISBN 1-875284-92-3

PSYWAR ON CUBA
The Declassified History of U.S. Anti-Castro Propaganda
edited by Jon Elliston
Newly declassified CIA and U.S. Government documents are reproduced here, with extensive commentary providing the history of Washington's 40-year campaign of psychological warfare and propaganda to destabilize Cuba and undermine its revolution.
ISBN 1-876175-09-5

HAVANA-MIAMI
The U.S.-Cuba Migration Conflict
by Jesús Arboleya
What were the origins of the 1994 "rafters crisis"? Why did the U.S. government decide that those Cubans would not be automatically admitted as they had been previously, and instead intern them at the Guantánamo Naval Base? How has this migration — and the Cuban émigré community — been used by Washington against Cuba since the 1959 revolution?
ISBN 1-875284-91-5

THE SECRET WAR
CIA Covert Operations against Cuba, 1959-62
by Fabián Escalante
The secret war that the CIA lost. For the first time, the former head of Cuban State Security speaks out about the confrontation with U.S. spy agencies and presents stunning new evidence of the conspiracy between the Mafia, the Cuban counterrevolution and the CIA. General Fabián Escalante details the CIA's operations in 1959-62, the largest-scale covert operation ever launched against another nation.
ISBN 1-875284-86-9